When Panda Was a Boy

A Collection of Stories on
Gender Identity for K-8

by Connie Dunn

10 Stories that Address GLBTTQ Issues
in a Gentle and Positive Manner
that also Helps Parents Talk to Their GLBT Children

When Panda Was a Boy, Copyright © 2014 Connie Dunn

Published by Nature Woman Wisdom

Published by No Stress Press

Printed in The United States of America

ISBN-13: 978-0615867670
ISBN-10: 0615867677
10 9 8 7 6 5 4 3 2

Library of Congress Cataloging in Publication Data

Dunn, Connie

When Panda Was a Boy

Gender Issues

When Panda Was a Boy

by Connie Dunn

Stories

When Panda Was a Boy

by Connie Dunn

My Gratitude for:

Barb Grieve, Heather Grant

All Religious Educators that Work with GLBTTQ Populations

All Children and Youth Who Identify as Gay, Lesbian, Bisexual,
Transgender, Transsexual, Trans or Questioning
and Their Parents

My Daughters: Michelle and Erin

My Wife, Joyce

Special Thanks to Andy Heller

Quilt Illustrations are original handmade quilts by Connie Dunn

Photography of quilts are done by Andy Heller of Heller
Photography (http://hellerphoto.com) in Attleboro, MA

Class, race, sexuality (sexual preferences), gender and all other categories by which we categorize and dismiss each other need to be excavated from the inside.

- Dorothy Allison

I love to be individual, to step beyond gender.

- Annie Lennox

TABLE OF CONTENTS

There isn't a theologian in the world who can argue with me on this. God has no gender. If that's the case, then everything needs to be rewritten now, right now.

- Susan Powter

DEAR PARENTS,

I first began thinking about these stories as a way to deliver diversity in a palatable manner to the kids in my Unitarian Universalist Sunday School program in Denton, Texas. At that time, I hesitated to go where these stories take you. Gender Identification is far more applicable to our children's lives than just making them gay and lesbian friendly. I am now retired from religious education, but the issue of gender identification still exists.

"Heather Has Two Mommies" was sensational when it first came out. But there were no stories about children who identify their gender in a different way. Many youth that I have known throughout the years have wanted something more than just male and female designation. For these children and youth, this is the set of stories that I have written for them, their parents, their children and grandchildren.

When I began writing these stories, I was not yet married to my wife. I was leaning toward lesbianism, but it took a long time for me to awaken to that identity. I was a trained facilitator for a comprehensive sexuality education program created by the United Church of Christ and the Unitarian Universalist Association, called *Our Whole Lives*. And I was also a youth advisor. That's when I met a group of teenagers who had been thrown out of their homes, because they were gay or lesbian.

It broke my heart to see these children abandoned, because they were seen as "monsters" by their parents. What must these kids be thinking about their own identities? The parents believed that their brand of religion had no room for gays and lesbians, even if they were their own children.

The stories in this collection range in age-appropriateness from Kindergarten to Eighth Grades. These are not stories about *coming out*, *sex change* or interest in adult sexual relationships. This is simply a collection of fictional stories where children raise question about their sexuality in innocent or in determined manners. These stories model how parents, grandparents, and other adults can be supportive of children, who may be exhibiting signs that they do not fit in the binary gender roles or typical heterosexual roles. Children need stories that support who they are!

Sincerely,

Connie Dunn

A BOY NAMED SUE

(Intersex – Gr. 4 & 5)

When Sue was born, his name was Stewart. His birth was fairly normal in all sorts of ways, except that he was born with what doctors refer to as *adrenal hyperplasia*, which means that externally he appeared to be a boy.

However, Stewart wasn't all boy. He also had the internal organs of a girl, which sometimes happens with this medical condition. It occurs in about one out of every 4,000 babies, which is more often than a lot of folks realize.

Shortly after Stewart was born, the doctors told Stew's parents that he was born with a condition, commonly known as *intersexed* or *intersexual,* and that there was a chance that Stewart would want to be a girl later in his life, but it was too early to tell if this would happen. "Not long ago," the doctor explained, "we would have just made a decision about which sex this child was going to be. In Stewart's case, we would probably have just left him like this with no surgery and suggested you raise him as a boy."

Stewart was the name on the birth certificate. And it also showed that Stewart was male – boy - baby. And this piece of paper just might make things complicated for Stew.

Sue lived as a boy with the name "Stew" or Stewart until he was five years old. But Stew knew he was different from the early age of two. He wanted to play dolls not cars.

He wanted to play house not wild horses. He would sit quietly and comb his *My Little Pony*'s hair and braid it. Mom and Dad saw this, as well. His favorite color was pink and he wanted to take dance and wear a pink tutu like all the other little girls his age.

When Stew was about to start the third grade, he wanted dresses and wanted to be called Sue instead of Stew. Mom wasn't sure what to do. She knew there was a chance that Stew was a Sue, and she had always given him both girl and boy toys. She had even let him take ballet and bought him the pink net tutu to play in!

But wearing a dress to school like all the other girls? Well, that was a different thing. He had been going to school as Stew. Mom had not been prepared to make this change, and certainly not so soon. But she took her cues from Stew and bought him dresses. Mom enrolled him in school with the name Stewart and the nickname "Sue."

"Mom," Sue said one day after school, "Some kid asked me why my name was Stewart and Sue at the same time. She asked if I was gay or something?"

"Sue," said Mom, "You are a very special person. You are both Stew and Sue at the same time. Most people are just a boy or a girl, but you are both."

Sue looked very confused.

"You are what doctors call *intersexed*. Boys usually have a penis and girls usually don't," explained Mom.

"I have a penis," said Sue.

"Yes," said Mom. "You do. But on the inside, you have girl organs not boy organs."

"Oh?" said Sue.

"This means that you are part boy and part girl, according to your body parts. But only you know who you are on the inside." Mom explained wondering if Sue would understand.

"I see," said Sue. "So I'm really Sue and Stew's a mistake?"

"I suppose you could put it that way," said Mom. "But when you were born, we had to choose between boy and girl, so we chose boy, because you appeared to be a boy."

"Are you mad that I'm Sue, instead?" asked Sue.

"No," said Mom, gathering her child into her arms. "I love you if you are Stew or Sue or both!"

Sue was happy that she could continue to be Sue. She had no idea that as she grew older surgery would be needed to change her outer appearance to reflect her feminine identity.

AMARA'S BIRTHDAY REQUEST

(Gender Questions – Gr. K-1)

Just before Amara turned six years old, she had learned quite a lot. She dressed herself in her own style each day. She even tied her own shoes! She knew where her eyes and nose and toes were. Her private parts also had names. She had a *vulva*, but boys had a *penis*.

On her birthday, she asked her Mom, "Can I have a *penis* for my birthday?"

With curiosity, Mom looked at her: "Amara," she said, "do you want a new elbow, as well?"

"Mom!" said Amara with her hand on her hip. "I have an elbow on each of my arms, but I don't have a *penis*."

"You have a *vulva*, instead," said Mom.

"I know," said Amara emphasizing her words with a pointed finger and a sway in her hip, "but I'm done with this whole girl thing."

"What do you mean?" asked Mom.

"Well," said Amara, "Kamal said that boys get to be sailors and explore the ocean. He said that girls can't do that. So…can I have a *penis* for my birthday?"

"Oh, sweet girl, we don't get to pick body parts from the toy store. That's a lot harder than you think," explained Mom.

But Amara was clear that she wasn't going to have it any other way than hers. Mom explained that girls can be sailors, too. "Girls can do just about everything a boy can do," said Mom.

"They can?" asked Amara as her eyes lit up. "Can I have a sailboat?"

Mom told her she could have a toy one for now, but when she got older, if she still wanted a sailboat, they would see if it was possible.

"Okay," said Amara.

Later that day when Amara was on the playground with Kamal, Amara said, "Hey, girls can do ever'thing a boy can do...like sail their own sailboat!" she said.

"No they can't!" yelled Kamal. "Girls aren't as strong as boys."

"Who said?" questioned Amara.

"I did!" said Kamal.

"Well, you're just some 'ol stupid kid," said Amara. "I know all there is to know about 'puters, do you?"

"Oh, yeah? "Kamal challenged. "I bet you don't even know what a 'puter is!"

"Do you?" asked Amara.

"Yeah, sure," said Kamal. "Every boy knows!"

"Well, when I get to be a boy, I'll do ever'thing better than you!" yelled Amara back to him.

"You're so stupid!" Kamal said. "Girls can't turn into boys!"

"Well! Then, you're gonna be real s'prised when I sail my own boat and use 'puters better than you, as well! And...I don't even need to be a boy to do that!"

BRAZOS DANCES

(Gay – Meaning – Gr. 3-6)

When Brazos started second grade, everyone asked him, "What kind of name is Brazos?"

He had liked his name. It was the name of the river near where his mother and father had met. But he didn't like getting teased. And to make matters worse, when he was just four-and-a-half years old, he had decided to become a dancer. He had seen Michal Baryshnikov, a famous American male ballet dancer, dance and he had wanted to dance just like him.

Boys, especially in Texas, didn't dance! That was, so it seemed, everyone's opinion at school—at least the opinion of the boys that Brazos wanted to be friends with. Brazos loved dancing with the same passion that other boys at his age loved soccer and baseball. He didn't dislike soccer or baseball or any other kind of ball. But he knew that dancing was what he wanted to do. And he knew his ballet classes were filled with girls, but he would even endure that. He was good at dancing, but a boy with a pair of ballet slippers in his backpack got teased quite a bit.

"Brazos is gay!" chanted a bunch of older boys.

Brazos cried. The words stung, but he really didn't know why or what they meant.

That afternoon when his mother picked him up from school, he asked, "Mom, what does 'gay' mean."

Mom looked long and hard at Brazos and answered, "Gay means to be happy, cheerful."

"Are you sure?" asked Brazos. "When some older boys called me 'gay,' today, I don't think they were saying I was happy. I was pretty sad. I even cried...and, you know, Mom, boys aren't supposed to cry. Is there another meaning, Mom?"

"Well," said Mom, "there is. It refers to when men and men live together like mom and dad. When they are life partners...just like Tom and Dillon, our next-door neighbors."

"Is 'gay' bad?" asked Brazos.

"Do you think Tom and Dillon are bad?" asked Mom.

Brazos shook his head. He remembered just day before yesterday when Dillon fixed his bike for him. And last week Tom helped him bake a cake. He liked Tom and Dillon. They were *cool* adult friends!

Brazos was puzzled. "Mom...if 'gay' isn't bad..."

"Brazos," Mom broke in, "some people think 'gay' people are bad. But they are just like everyone else. There may be a bad person who is 'gay', but that doesn't make all 'gay' people bad. Unfortunately, some people think people with dark skin are bad people. And though there are bad people with dark skin, it doesn't make everyone with dark skin bad. There are bad people with light skin, as well. There are good and bad people in the world. Now, let's talk more about what happened at school."

"The boys found out I had ballet slippers in my backpack. That's why they called me 'gay.' I took them for show-and-tell."

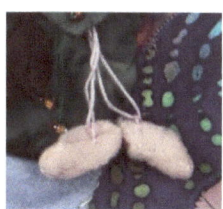

"Hmmm," said Mom.

"Mom, why don't other boys like me? Is it just because I dance?"

"I'm sure it isn't because you dance, dear. But boys who are ballet dances are not in the majority."

"Should I stop dancing?"

"Of course, not, dear!" Mom thought for a few minutes, then continued. "Dancing can come in many forms. Do you remember that you have a cousin who lives on a reservation in Oklahoma?"

"Yes, I remember Running Hawk. But what has that got to do with dancing?"

Mom reminded Brazos of his last visit with Running Hawk. He had gone to the reservation to visit and had learned to dance a ceremonial dance. Running Hawk's mother, who was Cherokee, had made Brazos some pants and a shirt to wear during a ceremonial dance. She had told him that to dance in the ceremony was an honor, and that such an honor deserved the appropriate dress. She had even made him a pair of moccasins to dance in. He had thought that the moccasins felt very much like his ballet slippers.

The very next *show and tell* day, Brazos took the moccasins to school in his backpack. When the older boys came to tease him about the ballet slippers, he showed them his moccasins. They were fascinated.

"Do you really wear moccasins?" the tallest boy, who was nine, asked.

"Only when I dance in ceremonial dances with my cousin, Running Hawk," said Brazos.

"Gosh!" said the other boy. "We wouldn't have teased you, if we knew you were an *Injun* dancer. You won't scalp us, will you?"

Brazos looked puzzled, then remembered an old movie he had seen where the *Indians* had scalped the *white* people they had killed. What had his mother called it? Oh, yes, she had said it was disgraceful. But, then, she had said it might have happened.

Brazos said, "I'm not *Native American*. But my cousin is half Cherokee. My Aunt Quill Worker made the moccasins for me. My father's brother, Uncle John, is Running Hawk's father. My uncle isn't *American Indian* either."

"Native American," said the taller boy in a mocking voice.

"That's what *American Indian* people should be called," said Brazos.

"You sure are odd!" said the other boy. "But maybe you're okay."

"Yeah," said the taller boy to the other one. "He may not even be gay, after all."

"I'm not!" protested Brazos. "I'm not even old enough!"

"What's that got to do with it?" asked the taller boy.

"Well, I'm not old enough to pick a life partner. My mom and dad were both 25 when they decided to get married," Brazos said.

"Oh!" said the two older boys.

"I'm not getting married," said the taller boy.

"Yeah, me neither," said the other boy. "You gotta like girls to get married!"

"Yeah," said the taller boy. "And you might just end up gettin' married to Elizabeth, who has red hair and freckles."

Brazos walked away from the boys feeling pretty good. He didn't think he wanted to be friends with the boys. He wasn't sure exactly why.

But he thought it was because they thought *Native Americans* might hurt someone just because they were *Native Americans*. He sort of thought these boys liked only the "not" nice parts of what they thought *Native Americans* were; and he was sure that this was not the way he wanted to be. He knew that there was much more to being an *American Indian* than some movies had shown where they were fighting the *white* man. Besides, his uncle had explained all that. The *Native Americans* were at war with *white* settlers, who were taking their land. There had been many wars. His dad had fought in the Persian war.

These boys were "bullies." Isn't that what he had learned from his Weekly Reader? Brazos did not want to be a *bully*, but he did not want kids to pick on him. He just wanted to be friends with kids. He wondered: "Am I really all that different from other kids?"

That afternoon when Mom picked him up from school, she asked how his day had gone. He asked her why some people were so mean about other people they didn't even know.

Mom explained, "Brazos, there are a lot of different kinds of people in the world. Some look different, because they come from different cultures, like Running Hawk is Native American, and you are not. Some believe differently, like we are Unitarian and believe that all people should be honored. Some people have other ethical values, which mean that they may not be honest, respect the earth and other people, or accept that there are many diversities in the world for which we are thankful."

"Mom, why do boys like the ones at school have to make fun of someone else or even a whole group of someone else's?"

"You have just learned a big lesson, today," said Mom. "It's easy to put someone or a whole group of people down so that you can feel better than they are. But standing up for who you are is a big job. Some people use physical violence, but you learned to resolve the problem with words instead. You also learned that words can be just as harmful as the physical violence. This is a big lesson, too! I think maybe you've even gotten taller!"

"Oh, Mom!" Brazos said playfully. "I'm not any taller! But I sure don't like some people that dislike people just because they think things that aren't even true."

"Learning the truth is hard, Brazos. Some people spend their whole life searching for truth only to find that their eyes were closed when the truth came to them," Mom said.

"Is that like the boys not understanding what was wrong with calling *Native Americans, Injuns?*" asked Brazos.

"Yes," said Mom. "Now get ready for your ballet lesson."

"Okay, Mom."

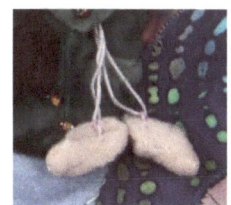

CHARLIE IS A GIRL

(Trans - Gr. 5-8)

Christina was looking at her reflection in the mirror. "This isn't the real me!" she said to no one. "I'm Charlie! I'm tired of looking at Christina." Christina pulled her hair back in a ponytail, pulled on jeans and a t-shirt. "That's better Charlie," she said to her reflection.

"Mom!" Christina called to her mom as she walked by her room.

"Christina?" said Mom.

"I want to talk. Is this a good time?"

"Of course, Christina, what's up?"

"Remember how we talked last summer about my wanting to be Charlie?"

"Yes," said Mom. "I remember. You were going to wait until you were going to Middle School in the Fall."

"Mom, I cannot wait! I hate me. I just have to start being Charlie, because I'm not Christina. I'm not sure I've ever been Christina."

"It's going to be a bit awkward to transition in the middle of the school year," said Mom trying to be as supportive as could.

"It's going to be more awkward, if I have to stay Christina!"

"I understand," said Mom. "Gender Identity is important to everyone...and more so for you. We'll need to talk to the principal."

"I'll talk to Mr. Morrow.

"Don't you want your dad or me to come with you?"

"It's my issue, Mom. I have to take responsibility for it. I've done some research. There is a law called AB537, which is

Federal Legislation that states no one can discriminate against anyone no matter what their gender identity is. They basically don't have a choice. Here, read this," she said handing Mom the paper.

AB 537 Fact Sheet (in part)

California Student Safety and Violence Prevention Act

What is your school district obligated to do?

If your school does not adequately address your complaint, you can take your complaint to your district superintendent's office (ask for the designated complaint officer or compliance coordinator). Your school district must follow the state's "Uniform Complaint Procedures," which say that your school district must to do the following:

• Have a staff member who is responsible for receiving and investigating complaints who is knowledgeable about the law.

• Every year, notify parents, employees, students, and anyone interested of the district complaint procedures, including the right to appeal the school district's decision to the California Department of Education.

• Protect you from retaliation after you make a complaint.

• Keep your complaint confidential as appropriate.

• Accept complaints from any youth, adult, public agency, or organization.

• Investigate your complaint, come up with a solution, and send you a written report no more than 60 days after they receive your complaint

What is the state Department of Education obligated to do?

As the authority over public schools, the California Department of Education (CDE) is responsible for making sure that schools follow AB 537. If your school district fails to adequately resolve your complaint, the CDE is obligated to do the following:

• If your school district does not act within 60 days of receiving your complaint or if you appeal the school district's decision, the CDE is obligated to complete an investigation within 60 days, and make a decision about whether the school district has lived up to its responsibilities and whether it needs to do anything else.

• Require schools to take steps to improve problems raised through investigation of complaints.

• Request a report of the schools' actions and keep a file of every written complaint received.

Go to AB537.org for more information

"Okay," said Mom, "I understand that the law is on your side. But that does not account for how people feel. Are you prepared for the fall out?"

"Mom," said Christina, "It can't be any worse than how I feel about 'Christina.' I need to be 'Charlie!' Do you understand, Mom? I…"

Christina's voice quivered as she stifled the tears that were just on the verge of pouring out..

"Your dad and I are behind you. How do you wat to go forward?"

"I'll go talk to Mr. Morrow tomorrow. I want to cut my hair and I want to talk to the doctor about taking male harmones, so I won't begin looking any more like a girl than I already do. I want to go to the gym and start doing some weight lifting."

"Chriii…Charlie, let's take this one step at a time. Talk to Mr. Morrow and make sure that they are going to cooperate. Law or not, the school officials can make this whole thing a lot more difficult if they fight you on it."

"I know you've been in counseling since last summer when you told Dad and I how you felt. Does Dr. Johnson support you in this transition?"

"Mom! I thought you believed in me and supported my decision!"

"I do, sweetie, I just want to make sure all the support is there for you. This is a rather big change. It doesn't happen to many kids. How are your friends and schoolmates going to react?"

"No one can predict that. Even if I wait until next Fall when I go to Middle School, Dr. Johnson told me that it wasn't possible to get a 'perfect' time."

"Okay," said Mom. "I'll be home tomorrow, so call me if you need me."

"Thanks, Mom. I really can handle this! I'm ready. I need to be Charlie. I've been Charlie my whole life, I'm ready to let him out!"

Mom smiled her approval.

The next morning, Christina, went to talk to Mr. Morrow.

"Hi, Mr. Morrow," said Christina. "I have something very important to talk to you about."

"Okay, Christina, what is so important?" asked Mr. Morrow.

"I want to change my name to Charlie and begin living my life as a male. I'm a transgender male. There is California Legislative Law AB537 that says I have the right to be me."

"I'm familiar with it," said Mr. Morrow. "Okay, Charlie?"

"Yes, Charlie."

Mr. Morrow held out his hand to shake Charlie's hand. "Charlie, welcome to Cherry Hill Intermediate School."

There was a bit of a pause, before Christina remembered one huge issue that she needed to negotiate before she came to school as Charlie. "Mr. Morrow, I think we need to talk about the restroom situation."

"Restroom?" asked Mr. Morrow.

"Well, Charlie is male. I cannot be going into the 'girl's' restroom."

"But it might be just as awkward that you are going into the 'boy's' restroom. Today, you are Christina. Tomorrow, you're Charlie. I don't think the boy's will be okay with you using their bathroom."

"So where can I go?"

"Charlie," said Mr. Morrow. I think the only choice is to give you access to the restroom down on the fourth grade hall. It has a key access. We don't want to get into a "bully" situation."

"Thank you, Mr. Morrow. Can I call my mom? I'd like to take the rest of the day off and get ready to come back tomorrow as Charlie."

"Let me say, goodbye, Christina. It has been a pleasure to have you at our school."

Charlie was beaming.

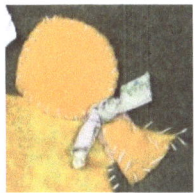

Charlie waited for Mom. He could hardly wait for her to come!

When Charlie climbed into the car, Mom asked, "Well, I take it that things went well?"

"Mom, it was fine, just like I said it would," Charlie said. "Can we go get my haircut and buy some "Charlie" clothes?"

Mom was pleased to see how enthusiastic Charlie was. She had seen Christina slipping into depression. "Yes, Charlie," said Mom.

Charlie grinned. Mom had never called him, Charlie!

DREW AND LESTER

(Gay – Gr. K-4)

Drew and Lester lived next door to each other. Their mommies were friends before they were born. Their mommies would say, "You were friends even before you were born."

Drew and Lester were born on the same day. Drew was born in the morning. Lester was born in the afternoon. They were best friends. They liked to play make believe and put on plays they made up instantly. They played well together and rarely ever had a disagreement.

When they were five years old, Drew and Lester began dance lessons. Drew and Lester loved to dance!

The girls wore pink leotards and tights. But Drew and Lester wore black stretch pants and white t-shirts. They had tap shoes and could make lots of noise.

Drew and Lester loved tap. Their moms took them to see "Tap Dogs," which was a tap company of men who tapped with water lights and lots of rhythm! The boys also took ballet; because it was required to make sure they built up their dance bodies in the right way.

Drew and Lester loved dancing. Their moms bought them lots of music of different kinds. Just about all sorts from Country Western and Rock to Classical!

The boys loved dressing up and dancing. They had all sorts of dress up clothes to go with all genres of music. But sometimes just their soccer tees and jeans worked fine! Drew and Lester also loved to sing while they danced.

Drew and Lester had both boy toys and girl toys. Sometimes they liked to have tea parties. Sometimes they liked to play with cars and trucks. When they had their sixth birthdays, they each got skates.

Still, Lester and Drew loved dance classes. The boys learned how to do leaps and turns in Ballet; and slaps, and kick-ball-change in Tap.

Their moms took them to the city to watch all kinds of dance. They loved watching the men leap high across the stage in Ballet and Modern dance. They even watched a dance troupe dance with poles.

Drew told their ballet teacher about the leaps they had seen. Lester asked if she knew how to do leaps. Their teacher smiled and taught them many leaps that would lead to higher leaps as they grew older and stronger.

Drew said, "I felt like I was flying."

Lester said, "Wow!"

At their annual recital, Drew and Lester got to show off their big boy leaps. Everyone cheered after they leaped across the stage. Lester and Drew beamed.

Drew and Lester got to tap dance together on stage, as well. They felt like *Tap Dogs*! Everyone at the recital loved them.

Drew and Lester loved each other. They grew up and became life partners.

EENY, MEENY, MINEY, MOE

(Trans/Genderqueer – Gr. 6-8)

Heather couldn't decide which *gender* she should pick on any given day. One day, she felt more male. Another day, she felt more female. But on some days neither gender seemed to fit.

When Heather got to college and went to work at Ferry Beach, a Unitarian Universalist camp and conference center, she shaved her head bald and pierced her nose. Some people wondered if she were girl or boy? And some days Heather wasn't sure herself. She had tried on both genders from time to time, but in the end she decided she was neither.

"Why do we have to have only two choices?" Heather asked. "I'd like to have a third category for something neutral, and I've been hearing others talk about *gender neutral.*"

"Why don't you pick like we did when we were kids coming here to camp!" suggested Kit, who loved the idea of choosing genders. He liked wearing skirts from time to time. He thought it might have been handed down from his Scottish relatives, who wore kilts.

To help move the decisions along, Kit burst into a little rhythmic ditty that he and Heather had made up their first year at camp and changed the words, of course, to match the gender question: "Eeny, meeny, miney, moe, which gender should I pick today: male, female, gender neutral, this is how we UUs (Unitarian Universalists) choose. Rock, paper, scissors. Rock, paper, scissors. One, two, three, four, five little UUs (Unitarian Universalists) sitting on the sand watching all the waves coming in and going out. Male. Female. Gender Neutral. Female, Male, Gender Neutral. Gender Neutral, Male, Female. Female, Male, Gender Neutral." Touching their hands together, Gender Neutral for Kit, and Male for Heather.

"Looks like you're Male today. I'll be Gender Neutral!" Kit announced to Heather.

"Can I borrow your work boots?" asked Heather. "I feel like dressing very butch!"

Lynn who had not participated in their selection process, but had heard the whole thing said, "Sweet! I'm female."

They all went about their duties at camp dressed as their chosen *gender*. No one said anything. It wasn't too surprising to anyone, because it was a Unitarian Universalist camp. Since UUs believe in the *inherent worth and dignity of every person*, the camp often saw males dressed in skirts and girls in decidedly male attire.

During one of the evening meals, the three of them were dressed in their chosen clothing for their *gender identities*, a boy, who was enrolled in the kid's camp, asked Kit, "So what are you supposed to be?"

Kit was used to answering straight forward, so he said, "I'm *gender neutral*."

"Oh!" said the boy. "What's that?"

Kit had to go into a long explanation for the child and wondered if his answers were okay.

Heather had a somewhat similar experience. "Are you a lesbian?" asked a girl named, Ginger, who was enrolled in the Middle School camp.

Heather answered, "Not today. I'm a male."

"How did you get to choose?" asked Ginger curiously.

"Me and two of my friends, who work here, did Rock-Paper-Scissors and selected what *gender* we would be," said Heather.

Naturally, that sparked some questions about how one could choose their *gender identity*. Heather answered all the girl's questions. However, Ginger was confused about *gender neutral*, which caused Heather to explaid further.

"If I chose to be *gender neutral*," asked Ginger. "How would I dress? How should people address me? I mean, you can't say *he, she* or *it* for pronouns. What do you do?"

Heather eagerly and calmly explained, "There are some new pronouns to use for *Gender Neutral* people. You can say: *Ze* for *he* or *she*; and *Zir* for *her* or *his*."

"Oh!" said the girl. "Then there is already something to use? *Ze...Zir...*I think I like this *Gender Neutral* language...that's my choice, too! You see! I'm not really a girl or a boy. I feel more like something in between."

Heather and the girl talked for a long while. Heather answered all her questions. The girl had never been clear what her *gender identity* was, but she knew she didn't fit well as a boy or girl. For the first time, Ginger felt she understood her own body.

Heather, Lynn, and Kit talked about Ginger and her questions. Kit and Lynn urged Heather to share in a workshop about her ideas surrounding *gender issues* and talk about the *gender neutral* language in hopes that more *Trans* children and adults might understand what was happening to them. It also helped people stretch themselves around *gender diversity.*

Heather did. And over the rest of the summer, she found literally a hundred or more people to share about *gender neutral* and how a third option should be available on all forms, birth certificates, etc.

When summer was over and the young adults returned to their homes in Massachusetts, they joined Mass Equality, which had worked to get equality for marriage passed. The organization was now in the process of promoting *transgender equality* and supporting legislation to be passed to prevent hate crimes.

As for Ginger, she grew up to be *Trans.* She, too, became an activist to help get legislation passed that would help the entire LGBTQ (Lesbian, Gay, Bi-sexual, Trans (transgender and trans-sexual) community.

GEORGE WANTS A DRESS

(Cross Dressing/
Transgender/Transsexual – Gr.K-6)

"Mom?" said George, who lives in the town of Buford with his mother, father, and sister, Sue.

"Yes, George," said Mom.

"Can I have a dress for school?" he asked, while playing with Sue's dolls that she had discarded nearly nine months ago.

Before Mom could answer, Sue said, "Boys are supposed to play baseball and football; or trucks and cars; not your sister's old dolls."

George preferred playing make believe with his action figures and Sue's old dolls or stringing pretty beads than playing sports. He was artistic not a sports kid!

Mom said, "George, we can shop for one."

"Boys don't wear dresses!" exclaims Sue. "All the boys will call you sissy! And they'll bully you!"

"Sue, don't be negative," says Mom. "If George wants a dress, we need to let him explore on his own. George, why do you want a dress?"

"Mom," says George in a calm voice that was more serious than his seven years, "My inside is a girl."

Mom and Dad talked it over. They knew that George approached life in his own way. Mom told Dad of a school where George would be more comfortable exploring his feelings – both inward and outward.

Dad said, "The new school sounds like a good idea. He'll be eaten alive in public school."

Mom took George to look at the new school. George met a boy wearing a pink frilly top and pink pants with a hat embroidered with the words: "Boys can wear pink, too!" The school had an art room with sculpting clay, paper and paints. George knew this was the school for him!

Mom and Dad enrolled George in the new school. George asked for a dress again. Mom took George shopping for a dress. He found a cute red plaid dress. He tried it on at home with knee-highs and tennis shoes.

Sue ranted to Mom, "I can't believe you're doing this to me! I cannot have a brother running around in a dress!"

"This doesn't affect you, Sue," said Mom.

"Mom, it's just strange having a brother who goes around wearing a dress!" whined Sue.

"Sue," Mom said, "We need to remember our first principle: the inherent worth and dignity of every person."

"I'm turning ten next month!" cried Sue. "I was hoping to have a party. But I can't invite my friends over with George looking like a girl. They all know I have a brother!"

Mom walked over to Sue and put her arm around her. "Sue, this is not about you," she said in her most comforting voice. "George is different than a lot of brothers. He's still your only sibling. Just because he acts more like a sister than a brother does not mean that your Dad and I love him less."

"But Mom!" Sue said in a bit more whiney voice than she intended, "It's embarrassing!"

"Are you saying that you're embarrassed by your brother?" Mom asked.

"Well, yes! That's exactly what I'm saying," said Sue.

"Ah," said Mom. "Then this is <u>your</u> issue!"

Sue pouted and was totally silent. Mom took advantage of the opportunity and continued, "Would you be embarrassed if your brother was deaf or blind or in a wheel chair?"

"Well, no!" said Sue still having trouble being reasonable or civil.

"Would you be embarrassed if your brother was mentally challenged?" Mom continued.

"No," Sue said.

"Then you're only problem with your brother is that you don't want him to be who he is," said Mom. "You know in early Roman culture men wore dresses and skirts and women wore pants. And in Scotland men wear kilts, which are just like skirts."

Sue thought for a few moments and in a much more rational voice said, "I see what you're saying. So, if my friends cannot accept George for who he is…maybe they're not really my friends?"

"Exactly!" said Mom.

I WANT TO MARRY A WOMAN JUST LIKE MY MOMMA

(Lesbian -Gr. K-4)

"Today is special!" Momma told Madison. "Rusty and Mollie Sue are going to church with us. Today, Rusty and Mollie Sue will get blessed, because it is the *Blessing of the Animals Celebration.*"

Madison was so happy that she clapped her hands.

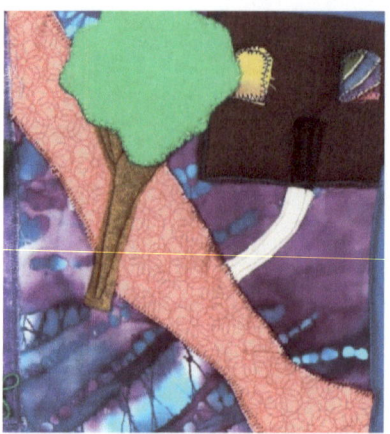

Once Church was over, Momma and Madison walk home with Mollie Sue, who was black and white, and Rusty, who was tan. Madison loved her Chihuahua doggies!

"Momma?" asked Madison, "Are Mollie Sue and Rusty married?"

Momma smiled, "No, but they love each other."

"Momma, when I grow up, can I marry a woman just like you?"

"I suppose you could, Sugar," said Momma, "if that's what you wanted to do?"

"Do Mollie Sue and Rusty want to get married?" asked Madison.

"Madison," said Momma, "Mollie Sue and Rusty are dogs. They don't really know understand marriage."

In her best seven-year-old manner, Madison said, "But that isn't fair! That's like Kaden!"

"What's like Kaden?" asked Momma.

"Kaden told me that girls only marry boys. Boys only marry girls! But Jane has two mommies! Curtis has two mommies and two daddies. Sierra only has one grandmother."

"Ah," said Momma. "Maybe I can help you sort things out."

"You can?" Madison questioned.

"Let's go back to your original question," said Momma.

"Can I grow up and marry a woman just like you?" Madison asked again.

"Yes," said Momma. "If you grow up and fall in love with a woman, then I expect that's who you were meant to be."

"Kaden told me girls always gotta marry boys!"

"Mm hmm!" said Momma

"Boys always gotta marry girls."

"Mm hmm!" said Momma. "Boys and girls do get married."

"But I don't like boys!" explained Madison.

Momma said, "Madison, sweet girl, you have a long time to decide who you want to marry. But no matter who you grow up and fall in love with, it'll be okay...man or woman...and that will be who you were meant to be."

"But Momma," Madison asked, "You married Daddy, and he's a boy!"

"Yes, Sugar," said Momma. "Momma and Daddy grew up and fell in love with each other. We got married and had a beautiful, curious girl just like you."

"But Daddy doesn't live with us anymore," said Madison.

"Oh, Madison! That's not your fault! Life is not perfect! We love who we love. Unfortunately, things happen in a relationship. Sometimes the adults decide not to be married any longer."

"Did you ever want to be married to a woman?" asked Madison.

"No, I didn't," said Momma. "But your Uncle Jerry fell in love with your Uncle Mike, and they love each other just as much as any other couple."

"Do Uncle Jerry and Uncle Mike have any kids?" Madison asked.

"Not yet," said Momma. "It's a big step to decide to have children. Maybe they just aren't ready yet."

"Momma," said Madison, "When I grow up, I really want to marry someone just like you!"

"Thank you, Sugar," said Momma. "I hope you find the sort of love you are hoping for. But that's not for a very long time. You have to finish elementary school, middle school, and high school, plus possibly college, before you're ready to fall in love and make a life-time commitment."

"Okay," said Madison, "As long as it's okay for me to marry a woman, I can wait 'til I grow up."

JUST CALL ME STEVE

(Gender Identity/Gender Bending – Gr. 3-6)

"Hey, girls don't play with footballs!" said Jill, who lived across the street from Stephanie.

"Why not?" questioned Stephanie. "I like football."

"It's a boys' game!" said Jill.

"So?" said Stephanie. "Girls can play football, too. There's even a National Women's Football Association."

Jill got quiet for a while as she studied every move Stephanie made. "That's not a girl's shirt," she blurted out rudely.

"I like it," said Stephanie. "Besides, I think I'm going to change my name to Steve."

"That's a boy's name!" said Jill.

"Well, I don't think I'm either a boy or a girl. Just call me, Steve!" she said.

"You are one crazy, mixed up girl, Steve!" said Jill.

"I don't think I like the term `girl' or `boy.' I think there ought to be something neutral," said Stephanie.

"We're about to turn 13!" said Jill remembering that their birthdays were two days apart. "Don't you want to date in a few years? Don't you want to do all that boy-girl stuff? I can hardly wait to have my first kiss!"

"By a girl or a boy?" Stephanie asked sincerely.

"A boy!" said Jill. "Have you gone off your rocker? There aren't any movie stars that are women who kiss women!"

"Yes, there are!" said Stephanie. "Ellen DeGeneres is a lesbian!"

"Shhh!" said Jill. "Our moms might hear you say that word."

"It's not a bad word," said Stephanie. "It's derived from *Lesbos*, a Greek island located in the East Aegean Sea where the ancient Greek lyric poet *Sappho* lived and ran a school for girls in the 6th century BC."

"What are you talking about? How do you even know this stuff?"

Stephanie took a deep breath and continued, "Many of her – Sappho's - poems are about her passion for her students. Sappho was the first person who connected love between females in her literature. This later led to the term *lesbian* having its modern meaning, as well as its rarer synonym *Sophism,* which means female homosexual or a female person who is sexually attracted to females.

"Omigawd!" yelled Jill. "I'm not sure what you just said, but I'm pretty sure we shouldn't be talking about it."

"What parts are you upset about hearing?" asked Stephanie.

"Well...like all of it, I guess!" admitted Jill. "You're talking about lesbian and homosexual and sexually attracted...I think my mom would pass out if I said any of those words where she could hear me."

"My mom helped me find these words and understand them," said Stephanie.

"Homosexuals are an abomination!" said Jill.

"Where'd you hear that?" asked Stephanie trying to control her frustration with Jill.

"From our minister," said Jill.

"Our minister says we should all stand on the side of love!" said Stephanie. "There are a lot of people who are sexually attracted to people of their same sex or gender. And there's nothing wrong with it. People are born being attracted to one gender or the other and it doesn't matter what gender they are. Some people are even attracted to both genders."

"Meow!" said Puffy.

"Puffy agrees," said Stephanie.

"Yeah, right! Puffy...who calls a male cat Puffy to begin with?" Jill said.

"Puffy doesn't mind. He likes his name!" said Stephanie.

"Uh, okay! But I'm not sure my mom will let us continue being friends," said Jill.

"Why is that?" asked Stephanie. "Are you afraid that I will want to marry you some day?"

"No. But it's just wrong," said Jill.

"Well, I'm not attracted to you. And if you truly feel this way, we were never friends. But if you want to talk to me, call me Steve; otherwise...it's been nice knowing you!" Stephanie exclaimed walking away.

Over Stephanie's shoulder, she called, "Oh, Jill, Puffy likes your blinged-out shoes...and other stuff!"

WHEN PANDA WAS A BOY

(Gender Identity/Gender Bending – Gr. K-2)

Panda lived in Lisa's trunk. It was a very soft place to live. Tiger, Monkey and Lizard were Panda's best friends.

When Lisa talked to Panda, he told her about when he was a boy. He talked about playing ball, and running fast, and making roads for his toy trucks.

Lisa wanted to be a boy, too. She hated lace. It itched and scratched. She liked soft pants and t-shirts best.

When Grandma came to play with her, Grandma made tea parties with Panda and Lisa with real tea in china cups. But Panda wanted to walk in the mud, so did Lisa.

Lisa left the china cups and Grandma in her special tea party hat. Lisa ran in all the mud puddles and showed Panda how to splash and jump.

"Why don't you play sweet games inside?" asked Grandma. "Why don't you act like a little lady?"

Lisa looked at Panda and back at grandma, "Panda was a boy, you know. I want to be one, too."

"But girls," said Grandma, "always like tea parties."

"I'd rather throw the ball," Lisa said.

"And what about wearing pink and pretty dresses?" asked Grandma.

"Pink?" said Lisa.

"Pink," said Grandma.

"I don't want pink!" said Lisa. "Give me blue or green! And let me have it soft like jeans and t-shirts."

"With pretty ruffles?" asked Grandma hopefully.

"I think I'm going to be a boy," said Lisa rather loudly.

"You are a girl, you know," said Grandma.

"Not anymore," said Lisa as she gathered up the `girl' items in her playroom. "I get to choose who I am inside. I am a boy!"

Grandma looked sort of sad.

"Grandma," said Lisa, "didn't you ever want to be a boy?"

"No," said Grandma.

"When Panda was a boy," said Lisa, "he was happy. I think I would be, too. Can girls be boys?"

"Girls can act like boys," said Grandma. "But girls are born girls and boys are born boys."

"Are they always?" asked Lisa.

Grandma thought a moment.

"No, Lisa," she said. "Some people are born girls who feel like boys on the inside. Some boys are born boys and feel like girls on the inside. Some boys like boys. Some girls like girls. And you are right. We must all be who we really are. Then we can be truly happy with who we are."

"Grandma, do you love me if I am a boy on the inside?" Lisa asked.

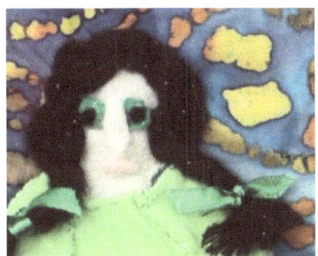

"Yes, Lisa," said Grandma. "I love you for who you are, even if you don't really know who you are, because I love the Lisa that is inside...down deep in your soul. Whatever is the essence of the true you...that's who I love."

"If I change my name to Max or Fred, would you still love me?" asked Lisa.

"Yes," said Grandma. "Your name is like a label. It isn't who you are."

"I think I feel like a Max," said Lisa.

"I love you if you are Max or Fred or Lisa, because I love you!" said Grandma.

Society as a whole benefits immeasurably from a climate in which all persons, regardless of race or gender, may have the opportunity to earn respect, responsibility, advancement and remuneration based on ability.

- Sandra Day O'Connor

MORE ABOUT GENDER ISSUES AND HOW I GOT INTO IT

A few years ago, I read a Ladies' Home Journal article about bullying and being gay. Many gay children were committing suicide, because of the bullying. Bullying continues to be a huge problem in our communities. It breaks my heart that our culture in America has produced an environment where bullying is so prevalent. We ARE in the 21st Century, aren't we? As a human race, I suppose I expect more of us. I don't know why? Clearly, we have not learned from our history of racial injustices. Crime soars in communities all across America and a large portion of that crime is labeled, "Hate Crimes." And too much crime is happening with our children and youth.

I saw a great deal of resistance in Massachusetts when the State Government was discussing a bill that would allow same-sex marriage. I stood behind police barricades and chanted with my daughter, Erin, at my side. She had been on the protesting line-up for weeks. A man approached me saying that my daughter was an abomination.

I admittedly was angry to hear this, even though I had heard my daughter tell me that this had happened repeatedly. I grabbed a woman who was standing next to me. I didn't know her, and she didn't know me. I put my arm around her and said, "If we want to be married and raise our children, it was our right." It didn't change that man's attitude. But I proudly stood my ground and professed my truest feelings. "People are people. Gays and Lesbians are people. Even, the man who called my daughter an abomination was a person. And transgendered people, who had barely gotten any recognition, were people.

Both of my daughters had come out to me as bisexual. I loved my children. Whether they were lesbians or heterosexuals or bisexual, and even had they been trans (Gender Neutral,

Transgender or Transsexual), they were still my daughters...my children.

The stories in this collection were designed to hopefully spark a discussion to open about gender in a kid-friendly manner. Parents can use these stories as a way of discussing this issue as a family. Many of the stories are based on some real facts - a collection of facts from numerous people. None of these stories depict an actual person or persons. This is simply a collection of fictional stories that are meant to help children feel normal about being who they are.

Only a few years ago lesbian and gay parents were not usually "out" at work. And that still may be the case in some places around the country. It is a bit harder to hide at school where both parents want to be involved in their children's school life, as they should be. As a result, lesbian and gay parents have to be creative in how they discuss this issue with their children, because of how they might be treated at school. Even now that gay marriage is legal in many states; there are people who are angry at gays and lesbians, not to mention adding transgender or transsexuals.

Not long ago there were no stories or books that could help a family, a classroom, etc. ease into this conversation. Mostly, there were lots of whispers between heterosexual adults, who were concerned what this would mean for their own children. Now same-sex couples are able to marry in a growing number of states. More people are aware that families come in all sorts of ways: single parents, heterosexual parents, grandparents, same-sex parents, parents where one or both parents are trans (transgender or transsexual). Even one legal man, who has given birth to now two children, has been in the news. His upper is man, but the lower part is still female, which allowed him to give birth.

In this book, I've mainly addressed the issues of children who may or may not have had some feelings and questions surrounding their own gender. Children may be born one gender, but may feel that the body doesn't match who they are inside or in their head.

These are difficult issues for families. Depending on what the religious background of the parents, there may be some ideas that their child is a "monster." But I believe in a God (or the mystery that some people call God) that would make no mistakes in creating people or the genetics that rule who each of us are with all our flaws and awesomeness.

Therefore, I set out to write a set of stories that addressed these issues in a positive way. I wanted parents to have stories they could use to explore these issues with their young children, especially those who have questions about these areas of their life. I believe that we should treat any gender issue as normal and address it in the most positive manner that we can.

Children as young as preschool may exhibit behaviors and preferences that clearly are out of the *norm* for heterosexual children, but are perfectly *normal* for lesbian, gay, bisexual or trans children.

(NOTE: I use the term Trans interchangeably for transgender and transsexual. Trans is the term used by some who feel gender neutral, or question the entire binary system, as well as those who feel their body does not reflect who they are. Transsexual refers to those who have surgically changed their gender.)

In the past, when babies were born with ambiguous genitalia or suffered from a botched circumcision, surgeons would just make a decision and have the parents raise the child as whatever seemed most doable. Creating a female out of a male child with a botched circumcision and expecting them not to have issues has been unreasonable. It was generally easier to fashion genitals into female. The parents then tried to raise the child as female. If that child didn't identify as female, then this became an issue for the family, the child, and for the community in which the child resided.

Doctors have stopped doing this and have recognized that this practice proved to be problematic for the children. Doctors now understand the issues that these children have. Previously, doctors felt that children grew up to be specific gender simply based on the environment in which the child was raised.

You can't just ignore these issues in your family. Parents do a disservice to their child, if they aren't supportive no matter what the issue is that arises. Parents don't always know how to react positively to their children that appear to be different from whatever the parents' belief system or experience might be. Often parents' and others' definition of *norm* is too limiting and not inclusive enough.

What I have created with this book is a set of stories that should help parents, teachers, and religious educators begin a dialogue to address gender issues with children. This allows the child(ren) permission to grow up to be the person - *male, female* or *trans* - that they are supposed to be.

As a Unitarian Universalist Religious Educator, *diversity* was and is one of the values that is both taught and embraced by this religion. However, not all families are Unitarian Universalist. Not all gays, lesbians, trans, or questioning children and youth are or become Unitarian Universalist (UU) either. No matter what the belief system is in your family, your first priority is your child. If you look further into your religion, you will hopefully find the strength to support your child(ren).

It was important for me to create stories that would help expand the diversity of humanity to include a wide range of possibilities that include all the possible sexual identities and preferences, because I want to give parents an opportunity to appreciate and bless the children they are given and not see them as "monsters," but as the special child that each and every child is.

Sophia Lyons Fahs, a Unitarian Universalist Religious Educator, said "No wise men see a star to point their way, to find a babe that may save humankind. Yet each night a child is born is a holy night." In other words, each child is a blessing and each birth makes each day holy not unlike the day that Jesus was born. Jesus was an important historical figure to most religious people in Christian, Jewish, Islamic, and Unitarian Universalists religions.

While my religion of Unitarian Universalism calls for me to embrace diversity and stand up for human rights, I also hear other religious people encourage "hate crimes" against people with gender identities outside of heterosexual identities. The laws are changing, but hate still resides in the hearts of people all across our country. It is my hope that we can begin healing from these divisions.

The bullying of children and youth, because they are gay must be stopped. It has driven many children to commit suicide. No child should be made to feel bad about who they are. Surely, humanity is not so archaic in their thinking that children should suffer due to who they are or who others *think* they are! Some of the children who have been driven to suicide were only "accused" of being gay and may not have actually been. There is too much hate in our country. I offer these 10 stories as an offering of peace and healing for all the children of this country and all around the world.

Kermit the Frog says, "It's not easy being green."

Heather Grant, a Unitarian Universalist young adult says: "When I am talking to someone, I'm not talking to their gender, I'm talking to them. When I love someone, I don't love them for their gender, I love them for who they are. Male, female, male to female, female to male, genderqueer, genderless, and all the other places inside or outside of gender and sex, why should it matter to me? Everybody is just beautiful."

I am sure that this will not be the last of my stories written on gender issues. At this time, I feel it is crucial to get these stories circulating and in use. Both parents and children need tools to help the discussion around these issues. Children are easily damaged when parents don't support their identity. Life is too short and too precious to waste time hating your child or at the very least uncomfortable with "who" your child is. Love them for who they are, even if it changes over time.

Enjoying your children should be your primary goal as a parent. I hope these stories help you discuss gender issues more openly. It is my thought that if we teach children to embrace other children that don't fit into the norm, we change the norm to be more diverse.

ABOUT AUTHOR CONNIE DUNN

Connie Dunn is an author, speaker, and educator. She specializes in working with fiction writers to help them get their book written and published. Connie writes both books and courses to help her students and coaching clients. She has more than 25 years of experience in writing for magazines and newspapers.

She had a regular column in the Dallas Morning News, which focused on small and home-based businesses. For this column, she won an award from the SBA (Small Business Administration). Connie also developed courseware for a number of start-up technology firms and with publishers, such as Prentice Hall Developmental (content) Editor.

She self-published her first book in 1981, and developed a collection of stories with a collaborator in the 1990s. She writes children's books, non-fiction, and fiction. Connie believes that everyone has a book in them and her greatest joy is in traveling with her students on their writing journeys.

Connie lives in Franklin, MA, with her wife, Joyce, and their plus-size cat, Sophie, and their tiny 5 $\frac{1}{2}$ pound Chihuahua, Rusty.

There's a gender in your brain and a gender in your body. For 99 percent of people, those things are in alignment. For transgender people, they're mismatched. That's all it is. It's not complicated, it's not a neurosis. It's a mix-up. It's a birth defect, like a cleft palate.

- Chaz Bono

GENDER IDENTITY DEFINITIONS

SOURCES: Oberlin University, Encarta, Wikipedia, and Harry Benjamin International Dysphoria Association

There are many new terms that parents and children who identify as non-heterosexual should probably get comfortable with hearing and using, as appropriate. Many of these terms go beyond the language in these stories, but may prove helpful to parents and children/youth that have gender identity questions or issues. Some terms are fluid and definitions change over time.

Adocate – Is a person who actively works to end the inequities , such as those of the GLBTQ community, as well as educate others about a group, such as the GLBTQ people

Ally – Is a person who is supportive of a group of people, such as allies for the GLBTTQ (gay, lesbian, bisexual, transgendered (trans), transsexual, questioning) communities. Allies generally attempt to educate themselves about the issues and support people who identify as GLBTTQ..

Androgyny – Is a person whose biological sex is not readily apparent, whether by chance or choice.

Asexual – a person who does not experience attraction (or very little) to either men or women

Assigned Sex or Gender – When babies are born, they are assigned a sex or gender based on an examination of the external genitals. In some cases where it is hard to identify as either gender (intersexed or adrenal hyperplasia or hermaphrodite), doctors used to assign a sex and tell the parents to raise the child as this gender and all would be well. However, experience says that doesn't work. More doctors are becoming sensitive to children's choices as they grow up. However, a gender is assigned on a birth certificate at birth.

Bi-Gender – Is when a person feels they have both a male and female side to their personalities. A newer term is Gender Neutral.

Binary Gender/Binary Sex – a traditional view of sex, which limits the possibilities to "female" and "male." This is now an outdated view of sex.

Bio-Boy – Is a term some people use to identify a man who was born male. This contrasts to transgendered men, who may have been born female and are in transition to being male. Transsexual is also a term used for anyone transitioning from one gender to the other.

Bisexual – a person who experiences sexual, romantic, physical, and/or spiritual attraction to both people of their own gender, as well as another gender. (This is often confused and used instead of "pansexual."

Closeted – a person who keeps their sexuality or gender identity or sexual attraction for someone of the same sex a secret from others; one who has "not yet come out of the closet."

Coming Out – this is the process for which people who are GLBTQ reveal their sexual preferences, sexuality, or gender identity to people in their life. NOTE: This is wrongly thought of a one-time event. It is often a lifelong process and may happen as a daily process. (Don't confuse this with "outing.")

Cross-Dresser – Is an individual who dresses in clothing that is culturally associated with people in the opposite gender or sex. While this behavior seems odd to the basic heterosexual crowd, most cross-dressers are heterosexual and conduct their cross dressing on a part-time basis. Cross-dressers cross-dress for a variety of reasons, including pleasure, a relief from stress and a desire to express opposite sex feelings to the larger society. Cross-dressing might also be termed gender non-conforming behavior. Cross-dressers may also be known as transvestites, but this term has fallen out of favor due to its psychiatric, clinical and fetishistic connotations.

DIY – Is a term used to describe those who perform some "Do It Yourself" transsexual transitioning, such as administering of hormones. This is done via the Internet, because hormone drugs are available by mail order. However, the FDA has warned that this is potentially dangerous. Careful monitoring of doses is required to assure a healthy process. Transitioning is a long process that includes living as the opposite gender or sex, going through psychiatric care and pursuing a series of medical surgical procedures.

Drag King – Is a biological female who dresses in masculine or male-designated clothing and can be a female-to-male cross-dresser. Drag Kings often identify as lesbians and many cross-dress for pay and for entertainment purposes in GLBT or straight night-clubs. A Drag King's cross-dressing is usually on a part-time basis.

Drag Queen – Is a biological male, usually gay-identified, who wears female-designated or feminine clothing. Many drag queens may perform in bars by singing, dancing or lip-synching, often for tips or for pay. A Drag Queen's cross-dressing is usually on a part-time basis. Some may prefer term of Female Impersonator.

Dyke – a somewhat derogatory slang term used to describe lesbian women; some lesbians have reclaimed this term and use it as a symbol of pride. It is more often used within a group of lesbians as an in-group term. It is more often used within a group of gay men as an in-group term.

Faggot – a derogatory slang term used for gay men; some gay men have reclaimed "faggot" as a symbol of pride. (

Female Impersonator - Is another term for Drag Queen.

Female to Male - This is a term that reflects the direction of gender transition. This may include a broad range of experiences, including those who identify male or men and those who identify as transsexual, transmen, female men or new men. There are some individuals who use the term MTM to underscore that while they were biologically female, they never identified as female.

FTM – FTM is an acronym, which stands for Female To Male.

Gatekeepers - Is used by the Gender Community to refer to psychiatrists, psychologists and other (usually) non-trans clinicians and providers who can effectively block trans people from obtaining hormones, surgery or related services needed for their gender transition.

Gender - Is a complicated set of socio-cultural practices whereby human bodies are transformed into men and women. Gender refers to that which a society deems masculine or feminine. Many articles have been written on gender; and there are countless definitions. But most contemporary definitions stress how gender is socially and culturally produced and constructed, as opposed to being a fixed, static, coherent essence.

Gender Bender - Is an individual who brazenly and flamboyantly flaunts society's gender conventions by mixing elements of masculinity and femininity. The gender bender is often an individual, who struggles to comprehend the social norms of gender, but chooses not to conform. For example, Boy George, a popular culture icon of the 1990s, was often referred to as a gender bender by the press.

Gender Dysphoria - Is a psychiatric term, which refers to a radical incongruence between an individual's birth sex and their gender identity. A gender dysphoric feels an irrevocable disconnect between their physical bodies and their mental sense of gender. For the most part, the Trans Community finds this term offensive or insulting, because it indicates that there is a psychological aspect to this. In actuality, this usually refers to adrogyne or hermaphrodite or intersexed. To embrace this term means that a person believes they are not mentally well; when in actuality they may be as well as anyone on the planet.

Gender Euphoria - Is a term coined by the Trans community to embrace their feelings of happiness and joy, because they are openly and proudly living in their preferred gender role.

Genderfuck – Not a term I like, but it is used by a lot of youth and young adults. It is when a person deliberately is sending mixed messages about one's sex, usually through dress (for example., wearing a skirt and a beard). This term or identity is often associated with contempt for gender binary standards, exhibited by the combining of extremes from male and female gender roles.

Gender Gifted – Is a term which refers to trans people and which calls attention to transgenderism as a gift rather than a curse. This term promotes diversity, challenges the status quo, and enriches both the trans individual and the society as a whole.

Gender Identity - Refers to an individual's self-identification as a man, woman, transgendered or other identity category.

Gender Illusionist – Is an individual who cross-dresses, often in a glamorous manner, in order to perform for pay in a nightclub or other entertainment venue. See also cross dresser, female impersonator, male impersonator

Gender Neutral – a term used to express a non-binary term for gender. There is male, female, and gender neutral.

Gender Neutral Pronouns – the whole problem with adding a third gender of neutral is that there are no pronouns. So...people have made up some choices: Ne, nem nir, nirs, nemself; ve, ver, vis, vis, verself; ey, em, eir, eirs, emself; ze/sie, hir, hir, hirs, hirself; ze/sie, zir, zir, zirs, sirself; xe, xem, xem, xyr, xyrs, xemself.

Genderqueer - A term which refers to individuals or groups who identify as genderqueer. For this population, the notion of being labeled as one sex or gender does not match the identities of the people or group. Genderqueers possess identities, which fall outside of the widely accepted sexual binary system. Genderqueer may also refer to people who identify as both transgendered AND queer. For example, who challenge both gender and sexuality regimes and see gender identity and sexual orientation as overlapping and interconnected.

Gender Neutral – Is a term used when you wish to avoid other categories of gender. Pronouns that are gender neutral include: zi and zir.

Gender Outlaw - A term popularized by trans activists such as Kate Bornstein and Leslie Feinberg, a gender outlaw refers to an individual who transgresses or violates the law of gender For example, one who challenges the rigidly enforced gender roles in a transphobic, heterosexist and patriarchal society.

Gender Role – Is a term that refers to the clothing, characteristics, traits and behaviors of an individual which are culturally associated with one of two genders: male/masculinity and female/femininity.

Gender Variant - Is a term which refers to individuals who stray from socially-accepted gender roles in a given culture.

This term may be used in tandem with other groups, such as gender-variant gay men and lesbians.

Genetic Girl (GG) – This term refers to a woman who was born female. It is used to differentiate a transgendered women from non-transgendered women. Some variation of this are: GW or Genetic Woman.

Genetic Woman (GW) – This term is the same as Genetic Girl or GG.

GLBTQ – abbreviation meaning Gay, Lesbian, Bi-sexual, Trans (Transgender/Transsexual) and Questioning.

GRS (Gender Reassignment Surgery) – This term is the preferred term in the Trans community for Sex Reassignment Surgery. See Sex Reassignment Surgery.

Hermaphrodite – Refers to individuals whose genitals are ambiguous or do not readily fit into male or female. See also Adrogyne or Intersex.

Homosexual – a medical definition for a person who is attracted to someone with the same gender. This is considered offensive/stigmatizing term by most members of the GLBTQ community.

Intersex – Refers to individuals born with genitals that show characteristics of both sexes or differ from their genetic sex. See also Adrogyne or Hermaphrodite.

Male to Female - This is a term that reflects the direction of gender transition. This may include a broad range of experiences, including those who identify as female, women, transwomen or new women.

MTF - MTF is an acronym which stands for male-to-female.

Outing – This term is used when someone reveals another person's sexuality or gender identity to an individual or group, often without the person's consent or approval. (Do not confuse this with "coming out.")

Packing - Is a term used for people who are wearing a dildo, strap-on, or penile prosthesis. Sometimes used by female-to-male, cross-dressers or transmen.

Pansexual - a person who experiences sexual, romantic, physical, and/or spiritual attraction for members of all gender identities/expressions.

Pass - Gendered passing refers to an individual's ability to be regarded by others in accordance with one's preferred gender role in a socio-cultural context. For instance, a biological male who has a female gender identity and lives in a female gender role is able to "pass" as a woman to the people who surround her. This might also refer to race issues where one passes as another race, as in a light-skinned Black person passing for White. Or for a Gay man passing for heterosexual.

Queer - historically, this is a derogatory slang term used to identify GLBTQ people. However, this term has been embraced and reclaimed by the GLBTQ community as a symbol of pride. This term is representing all individuals who fall out of the gender and sexuality "norms."

Questioning - This refers to the act of individuals who are exploring their own sexual identity or orientation/affinity, investigating influences that may come from their family, religious upbringing, and/or internal motivations.

Read - To be read is to the opposite of passing. When a person is read, then someone is able to detect that you are transgender, i.e. your assigned birth sex does not match your preferred gender role/expression.

Real Life Test - This term is an assessment term which refers to the period of time when a transperson begins living "full time" in their preferred gender role to when they are considered "good" candidates (by psychologists, psychiatrists and others) for sex reassignment surgery.

Same Gender Loving (SGL) – a phrase coined by the African America/Black queer communities used as a alternative for "gay" and "lesbian" by people who may see those as terms of the White queer community.

Sex - Separate from gender, this term refers to the cluster of biological, chromosomal, and anatomical features associated with maleness and femaleness in the human body. Sex is often used synonymously with gender in this culture. Although the two terms are related, they are defined separately to differentiate between biological sex and sociocultural gender.

Sexual Affinity/Sexual Orientation – These terms refer to the gender(s) which a person is affectionally, emotionally, romantically and physically attracted to. Examples of sexual orientation include: homosexual, bisexual, heterosexual and asexual. Trans and gender-variant people may identify with any sexual orientation, and their sexual orientation may or may not change before, during or after gender transition.

Sexual Dimorphism - This term used with humanity is often thought to be a concrete reality as in the physical difference between external genitals. However, in reality the existence of intersex people points to a multiplicity of sexes in the human population.

Sex Change Operation - This term is often used as synonymous with sex reassignment surgery.

Sexual Preference – This term is generally used to mistakenly interchanged with "sexual affinity" or "sexual orientation." This term creates the illusion that a person has a choice or "preference" in who they are attracted to.

Sex Reassignment Surgery - This term is used to explain the operation(s) and procedure(s) which physically transforms the genitals using plastic surgical methods. The MTF surgical procedure is called a vaginoplasy. The FTM surgical procedure is called genitoplasty or Phalloplasty. The FTM transition also requires breast reduction surgery, where the breasts are basically removed and nipples sewn back into place.

Sexuality - Sexuality is a broad term which refers to a cluster of behaviors, practices and identities in the social world. All people are born as sexual beings much like people also have a spiritual side. It just depends how we view these aspects within ourselves.

Sexual Orientation/Sexual Affinity - These terms refer to the gender(s) which a person is affectionally, emotionally, romantically and physically attracted to. Examples of sexual orientation include: homosexual, bisexual, heterosexual and asexual. Trans and gender-variant people may identify with any sexual orientation, and their sexual orientation may or may not change before, during or after gender transition.

SOFFA - Is an acronym that stands for Significant Others, Friends, Family and Allies. This term is used to indicate those persons involved in the gender community because of their supportive relationship to a trans person.

Standards of Care (SOC, officially the Harry Benjamin Standards Of Care) - This is a series of guidelines for doctors and health professionals for deciding who qualifies to have hormones and surgery. While this remains controversial within the transgender community, the guidelines were meant to standardize the method by which transsexuals came to their decision and what steps the patient needed to make to psychologically prepare for this transition.

Trans – This is an umbrella term which refers to cross-dressers, transgenderists, transsexuals, genderqueer and others who permanently or periodically dis-identify with the sex they were assigned at birth. Trans is preferable to transgender to some in the community because it does not minimize the experiential specificities of transsexuals. See Transgender.

Transgender (TG) – A range of behaviors, expressions and identifications which challenge the pervasive bipolar gender system in a given culture. Transgender was originally a word coined to describe individuals who desired to change their gender expression without making hormonal or surgical changes to their bodies. While retaining its use as an identity descriptor for some, it has also evolved into an umbrella term including many categories of people who transcend traditional gender roles. This can include (but is not limited to) people who identify as transsexuals, cross-dressers, masculine-identified females, feminine-identified males, twospirit people, MtFs, FtMs, bearded women, transmen, transwomen, and other differently gendered people. Transgender people come from every race, class, sexual orientation, and ability.

Transition – This refers to the period of time in which a person begins to live in a gender role which is in accordance with their internal gender identity. This could include, for instance, the period of time when a person assigned female at birth who has a masculine gender identity begins to live in the role by dressing as a man, taking testosterone therapy, and/or getting surgery. Likewise for men transitioning to women, this is generally the time that it takes to live in the role and go through all the surgical procedures. Some transgendered/transsexuals do not go through all the surgical procedures at once or ever. It is very expensive to transition. It is not a choice that should be taken lightly.

Transphobia - This is a term used for those who fear and hatred of all those individuals who transgress, violate or blur the dominant gender categories in a given society. Transphobic attitudes lead to massive discrimination, violence and oppression against the trans, drag, and intersex communities.

Transsexual (TS) - An individual who strongly dis-identifies with their birth sex and wishes to utilize hormones and sex/gender reassignment surgery as a way to align their physical body with their internal gender identity. Some persons prefer the alternate spelling of transexual (one "S" instead of two).A TS can be MtF or FtM. He or she can also be pre-operative (pre-op), post-operative (post-op) or not intend to have an operation (nonop.)

Two-Spirit - A Native American person who embodies both masculine and feminine genders are referred to as being Two Spirited People, which is a much stronger and positive term than many. Native Americans who are queer or transgender may self-identify as two-spirit. Historically, different tribes have specific titles for different kinds of two-spirit people. For example, the Lakota tribe includes Wintke, the Navajo tribe refers to some individuals as Nedleeh, and in the Cheyenne tribe some two-spirit people are known as Hee-man-eh.

Thanks for Reading!

THE END